Space and Time

Ypsilanti, Michigan

Related Resources From High/Scope® Press

High/Scope Educational Research Foundation. (2003). *Classification, seriation, and number* [booklet].

High/Scope Educational Research Foundation. (2003). *Classification, seriation, and number* [videotape].

Hohmann, M. (2002). *A study guide to educating young children: Exercises for adult learners* (2ⁿᵈ ed.).

Hohmann, M. & Weikart, D. P. (2002). *Educating young children: Active learning practices for preschool and child care programs* (2ⁿᵈ ed.).

Published by

HIGH/SCOPE® PRESS

A division of the High/Scope® Educational Research Foundation
600 North River Street
Ypsilanti, Michigan 48198-2898

Orders: By phone, (800)40-PRESS; by fax, (800) 442-4FAX; online at *www.highscope.org*

Booklet Writer and Editor: Linda Koopmann
Graphic Designers: Linda Eckel; Kazuko Sacks, *Profit Makers LLC*
Photographer: Gregory Fox

Library of Congress Cataloging-in-Publication Data

Koopmann, Linda, 1946-
  High/Scope preschool key experiences. Space and time / High/Scope Educational Research Foundation ; [booklet writer and editor, Linda Koopmann].
     p. cm.
  Includes bibliographical references.
  ISBN 1-57379-145-8 (pbk. : alk. paper)
  1. Mathematics--Study and teaching (Preschool) 2. Space perception.
3. Time perception. I. Title: Space and time. II. High/Scope Educational Research Foundation. III. Title.
  QA135.6.K69 2004
  372.7--dc22
                          2004005755

Printed in the United States of America

Key Experiences in Space

Key Experiences in Time

How do young children learn <u>math</u>?

Young children are *active* **learners** who learn math concepts by pursuing their own interests while being actively supported and challenged by adults. As children wonder about what things are like and how things work, their curiosity leads them to explore their environment in search of answers.

Young children are also *concrete* **thinkers**. In contrast to adults and older children who can use abstract methods such as paper-and-pencil arithmetic or mental calculations to solve math problems, young children first need to see objects and physically work with them before coming to their mathematical conclusions.

What are High/Scope's thoughts on teaching math to young children?

Educators have long debated about when and how to introduce mathematics to young children. Some educators, as well as parents, believe that preschoolers are too young for math in any form. Others believe they should be taught counting and basic arithmetic before beginning elementary school. **High/Scope takes a balanced position in this ongoing debate and is involved in discussions with leading experts in the field.**

Young children are naturally curious about math and need to hear math-related language and have math-related experiences throughout the day. Our job as teachers and parents is to provide them with the words, materials, and experiences appropriate for math learning at their age so they can investigate size, quantity, categorization, patterns, space, speed, and sequence on their own terms with our support and encouragement.

Recognizing and capitalizing on math opportunities throughout the day **requires planning, systematic thought, and a willingness to enter your children's world on their terms and with their points of view in mind.** As you develop successful strategies to support their emerging skills in space, time, and other areas, **focus on providing an active learning environment, a consistent daily routine, and positive teacher-child interaction.** As part of the daily routine's **plan-do-review process,** allow children to **make choices** about what they will do, to **carry out their ideas,** and then to **reflect on their activities** with adults and peers. And make sure that blocks of time in the daily routine are long enough for children to play uninterrupted.

High/Scope's math-related key experiences for early childhood

High/Scope has identified **23 math-related key experiences** for early childhood—six in *space,* four in *time,* seven in *classification,* three in *seriation,* and three in *number.* (The classification, seriation, and number key experiences are covered in a separate booklet in this series.)

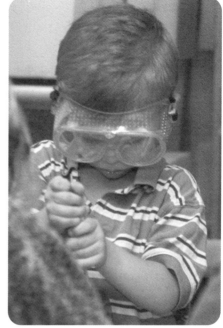

Young children learn about math concepts by exploring their environment and working with a variety of materials.

Adults can encourage math learning by providing children with the materials, experiences, and math language appropriate for their age.

The plan-do-review process allows children to make choices, carry out their plans, and reflect on their experiences later with adults and peers.

As they observe and join children at play, teachers in High/Scope settings try to understand each child's unique and developing ability to reason and understand *space* and *time,* as well as other math concepts. They then adjust their support strategies to accommodate these emerging skills. They also recognize the importance of valuing and accepting children's explanations for their findings, even if some of them don't quite fit within adult standards.

In the following pages are descriptions and anecdotal examples of each math-related key experience in *space* and *time* and suggestions for supporting each one.

Teachers in High/Scope settings tailor their strategies to support each child's unique developing abilities.

The key experiences in *Space*

As infants, children experience how things move through space by watching parents, siblings, pets, cars, bikes, toys, and other objects move from one place to another. As they learn to crawl, scoot, or toddle, children move through space on their own in search of people, toys, and other interesting objects and experiences. As preschoolers, children move through space with confidence in more daring ways than they could as toddlers, by climbing up a ladder, sliding down a slide, sledding down a hill, and running down the sidewalk. They fit puzzles together and take them apart, and arrange blocks in tall stacks and knock them down.

As they play, preschoolers use their increasing command of language to talk excitedly about their favorite experiences with spatial relationships. And their ability to form mental images lets them represent spatial scenes from memory with markers, paints, scissors, or balls of clay.

The six *space key experiences* present a composite picture of things preschoolers do that enable them to understand simple spatial relationships.

In the following pages we discuss each of the key experiences in space and provide suggestions for supporting each one.

Key Experiences in Space

Involving actions on objects:

★ Filling and emptying

★ Fitting things together and taking them apart

★ Changing the shape and arrangement of objects (wrapping, twisting, stretching, stacking, enclosing)

Involving actions as well as observations and interpretations about space:

★ Observing people, places, and things from different spatial viewpoints

★ Experiencing and describing positions, directions, and distances in the play space, building, and neighborhood

★ Interpreting spatial relations in drawings, pictures, and photographs

★ Filling and emptying

Preschoolers enjoy the simple act of filling a space or container and emptying it again. Such simple experiences provide a concrete example of how adding or removing material changes the amount of space available for filling. Children eventually learn that to create more space for filling, they either must remove something from the container or find a bigger container.

Examples of children
Filling and emptying

- DeJuan pours dry macaroni into a large pot, "cooks" it, and spoons the cooked macaroni into small bowls.

- Kyoko pours colored water through a funnel into a bottle until it spills over the sides. Then he pours some out and fills the bottle again until it just reaches the top.

- Danae dumps blocks out of a container and fills it with colored scarves.

Joining children at work offers adults many opportunities to support them with math language they can understand.

Ways to support children in filling and emptying

- ● ● ● ● ● ● ● ● ● ● ● ▶ *Provide materials for filling and emptying.*

An indoor sand and water table and an outdoor sandbox close to a water spigot or pump will allow children to fill a variety of containers with sand, water, salt, or flour and empty them again in a way that is easily cleaned up at cleanup time. Small collections of familiar things, such as plastic animals, beads, poker chips, shells, and pebbles, are also fun to use for filling and emptying. A convenient list of these and other suggested materials to use for filling and emptying activities is provided on p. 38.

Two boys work together to fill a large container with small colored blocks.

- ● ● ● ● ● ● ● ● ● ● ▶ *Watch for and comment on children's filling and emptying play.*

Children can be observed filling and emptying things in many areas other than at the sand and water table and sandbox. You can also watch them as they wash dishes or paintbrushes at the sink, fill and empty cooking pots in the house area, and empty and re-fill whole containers of blocks or small toys. As you observe, listen for language that indicates children's early understanding of spatial relationships. Expand their vocabulary as you comment on their play, for example, with words and phrases such as "full," "empty," "making more room," "less space," and so on.

- ● ● ● ● ● ● ● ● ▶ *Imitate children's actions.*

Join children's filling and emptying play at their physical level by kneeling, sitting, or pulling up a chair. Find your own container and filling materials and do what the child is doing. As children see that you are taking cues from them, they often initiate conversations about what they are doing or even about an unrelated topic.

- ● ● ● ● ● ● ● ● ▶ *Anticipate repetition.*

The sound, sight, and touch sensations associated with filling and emptying activities are very soothing for children, just as they are for adults. You will often find young children repeating these activities throughout the day as a way to seek comfort, as well as a way to explore and create or to socialize with other children around a satisfying task.

★ Fitting things together and taking them apart

Like the filling and emptying activity, fitting things together and taking them apart again offers young children spatial challenges and a sense of accomplishment. Putting puzzles together, zipping zippers, and building things with Tinkertoys are examples of fitting and taking-apart activities that help children solve problems through trial and error.

Examples of children
Fitting things together and taking them apart

- Liu fits all the pieces of a puzzle together, takes them apart, and puts the puzzle together again.

- Lakeisha makes a large square out of long wooden blocks and fills the square space with other blocks positioned side by side.

- Jennifer screws nuts of different sizes into bolts of corresponding sizes.

Toys with interchangeable parts offer children endless possibilities for fitting things together and taking them apart.

8

Ways to support children in fitting things together and taking them apart

• • • • • • • • •▶ *Provide materials that fit together and come apart.*

Stores and your own home offer such a wide variety of materials children can use to fit pieces together and take them apart again. For example, you can purchase many kinds of interlocking blocks, snap-together trains and train tracks, dolls and doll clothes, and trucks and cars with removable parts. At home you can collect boxes and plastic containers with lids, pots with lids, coffee percolators, and sets of screws and nuts. A convenient list of other suggested materials to use for fitting together and taking apart activities is provided on p. 38.

• • • • • • • • •▶ *Provide materials children can use to make their own things that fit together and come apart.*

As children gain skill with taking things apart and fitting things together, they also enjoy making their own things that come apart and go back together. A list of art and woodworking materials that allow them to do this is provided on p. 38.

Children can use clay, play dough, and other art and woodworking materials to make their own fit-together, take-apart things.

• • • • • • • • • •> ***Provide time for children to work with materials on their own.***

Just as we need time to figure out how something comes apart or fits together, children need time to experiment with materials through trial and error. Resist the urge to hover over children, instructing them on how to do it "right." But feel free to join them in their play by gathering similar materials and imitating their actions. Sometimes, interesting conversations will naturally arise between you and children during a pause in your side-by-side activities.

• • • • • • • • • •> ***Support children as they solve fit problems.***

Although children are generally resourceful in solving a problem when left to figure it out by themselves through trial and error, at times nothing they try works, and they become frustrated. Adult support at this point can help them overcome

Children can usually solve fit problems on their own if given enough time.

frustration and follow through on their intentions. In the following situation, Terry, the adult, suggests an alternative to Brianna that allows her to carry on with what she was doing:

Brianna: *I CAN'T GET THIS DUMB THING TO STAY ON!*

Terry: *You're trying to fit a top on that narrow bottle, and that one seems too large. It won't stay on.*

Brianna: *Yeah...maybe there's a smaller one in this bucket.*

• • • • • • • • • • ► *At recall time, encourage children to talk about things they put together and took apart.*

Here are the kinds of things you might say to encourage children to remember their experiences and talk about them during recall time:

• "Today I saw Ben take apart his truck and put it back together again."

• "Jamal made a very big tower with Tinkertoys."

• "I noticed Luisa putting on lots of jewelry in the house area during work time."

Watch children at work time. Give them cues at recall time to help them remember what they did.

• • • • • • • • • • ► *Include fit-together, take-apart materials at small-group time.*

Provide each child at small-group time with identical or similar sets of take-apart, put-together materials and watch how they experiment with how things fit. Children enjoy not only their own explorations but also the different ways in which other children in their group explore and experiment with the same materials.

11

Key Experience

★ Changing the shape and arrangement of objects (wrapping, twisting, stretching, stacking, enclosing)

Through this key experience, children learn firsthand that many materials can be reshaped and rearranged while remaining essentially the same as they were. For example, a piece of play dough can be rolled into shapes that look very different, but children know that all of the shapes are still made of play dough. Many such materials can be returned to their original shape.

Examples of children
Changing the shape and arrangement of objects

- Alex gathers all the dominoes into a big pile and then rearranges them into a neighborhood of roads for his toy cars.

- At snack time, Roberto arranges all of his crackers in one tall stack and then rearranges them into stacks of two.

- Martina twists two scarves together and tries to tie them around her waist.

- Stella, the teacher, and three children rearrange the book area. They transfer the magazines from the bottom shelf to a plastic milk crate and move one of the beanbag chairs from the house area to the book area. "Now we can cuddle together while you read to us," says Callie.

A well-stocked preschool setting provides many materials that can be wrapped, twisted, or stacked.

12

Ways to support children in changing the shape and arrangement of objects (wrapping, twisting, stretching, stacking, enclosing)

• • • • • • • • • ▶ *Provide materials to shape and arrange.*

Most of the materials in a High/Scope preschool setting can be arranged and shaped by children.

See p. 39 for a summary list of these materials.

• • • • • • • • ▶ *Support children as they rearrange things to solve problems.*

As we mentioned earlier, children can often solve their own problems when they are left to figure things out by themselves. As children explore possible solutions through trial and error, adults can support them by

• Observing their efforts to solve spatial problems

• Giving them time to try out a number of potential solutions

• Joining in their play and following their instructions, for example, by holding the end of a board or moving a block into place while the child lifts up another block.

These girls have arranged blocks to create a cozy and protected space for building tall towers.

13

➤ *Listen for children's awareness of how they are shaping and arranging things.*

As children shape and arrange materials, they sometimes indicate an awareness of the changes they are making by commenting on them:

• "Here, Miss Keisha. I made this for you. I had to scrunch it up to make it fit [in the envelope]."

• "When I do this [rolling a scarf into a long cylinder], it looks like a snake. But when I go 'Presto' [letting the scarf fall to the ground], it disappears."

Listening to children converse as they shape and arrange things may give you insight into their ability to understand spatial relationships.

➤ Take cues from children to comment on changes they have made.

When children bring objects to you that they have shaped, re-shaped, or arranged, support and encourage them by commenting on what you see and the changes children have made. For instance, you might respond to the above examples in the following ways:

- "Thank you! You sure made it fit in the envelope!"
- "Looks like you're making magic!"

Joining children as they play, as well as following their lead, offers opportunities for spontaneous conversation about how shapes are changing.

This child is intent on changing the shape of the piece of wood she's drilling.

Key Experience

★ Observing people, places, and things from different spatial viewpoints

Who doesn't remember hanging upside down from a climbing structure as a child? How different the world looked from that position. As preschoolers move easily through space, they get themselves into all kinds of new and unusual positions, and these positions offer them important new perspectives on how things relate in space.

Examples of children

Observing people, places, and things from different spatial viewpoints

• Taylor looks through the binoculars and takes "pictures" of his classmates.

• Dakota and Evan lean back in their swings and observe the rest of the playground. Evan says, "Look, the trees are standing on their heads!"

• Ayesha and Jane hide under a corner table and watch as Francesca tries to find them.

• Jeremy lies on his back under the table and looks at how the legs are held in place by screws.

Children love to hang upside down.

16

Ways to support children in observing people, places, and things from different spatial viewpoints

● ● ● ● ● ● ● ● ● ● ▶ *Provide sturdy play equipment.*

Provide sturdy outdoor equipment that lets children climb and change position, such as swings, climbers, climbing nets, tree stumps, merry-go-rounds, ladders, hills, bridges, slides, tree houses, tunnels, seesaws, wheel toys, tricycles, scooters, a sand pile, and large inner-tubes. Provide indoor equipment such as large sturdy blocks, cardboard boxes, stools, a small stepladder, large floor pillows, a rocking boat, and a hammock.

The world looks much different from the top of a play structure.

Encourage children to crawl, roll, bounce, and lie on their backs.

Most children need little encouragement to crawl, roll, bounce, or lie on their backs. Others need to be encouraged to move in many different ways so they have the opportunity to notice how things look from different physical levels. Work these kinds of movements into activities throughout the day—during transitions, small-group time, large-group time, and outside time. For example, cover the underside of your small-group tables with butcher paper and cover the floor under the table with pillows so that children can enjoy lying on the pillows and drawing with markers on the paper above them.

Activities that encourage children to see things from different spatial viewpoints can be worked into all times of the day.

▶ *Join children in a variety of positions.*

Get in touch with your childhood memories of viewing the world from different positions by joining children as they go down the slide, lean backwards over a chair, or lie on their backs in the grass while gazing up at a tree branch. Seeing things from their point of view provides natural conversational opportunities such as this one between Susan, a teacher, and Midori:

Midori [stretched out on the classroom floor]: *I'm a lady bug. Lady bugs can't see what's on the table.*

Susan [stretched out on the floor next to Midori]: *We can't see what's on the table or what's sitting on the chair.*

▶ *Take walks with children.*

Walk with children through the neighborhood near your preschool during small-group, large-group, or outside time. Listen for comments they make as they look at things from different viewpoints:

Thomas [as they approach and walk past an interesting building]: *That building just grew up. I can't hardly see the top.*

Mary [intently watching a figure approach and laughing as it passes by]: *That looks like my mom! No, it's not my mom—it's a man!*

Join children as they explore spatial relationships so you can see things from their perspective.

Key Experience

★ Experiencing and describing positions, directions, and distances in the play space, building, and neighborhood

As preschoolers explore and play in familiar environments, they experience and begin to describe *positions, directions,* and *distances* in ways that make sense to them. Their *verbal descriptions* of these experiences will also make sense to them, even if they are incorrect by adult standards. In an active learning setting, children feel free to try out spatial language without fear of correction or ridicule. In time and after lots of experimentation, children will begin to understand abstract spatial concepts and begin to use spatial language more appropriately as they describe their experiences.

Examples of children

Experiencing and describing positions, directions, and distances in the play space, building, and neighborhood

• "First you put the ice cream in the bowl, then you pour chocolate on it, and you put a cherry on top, and I put nuts on mine, too," says Matthew as he describes the sundaes his family made the night before. (Position)

• "Mr. Ryan, if we go that way we'll go by my friend's house," says Diane as she walks in the neighborhood with her class. (Directions)

• "No, that's too far. You've got to stand right here," Darius directs Ramona and Tony as they play a kicking game with a ball. (Distance and position)

"I'm taller than everyone. Now I'm gonna jump."

Ways to support children in experiencing and describing positions, directions, and distances in the play space, building, and neighborhood

●●●●●●●●●▶ *Provide materials children can set in motion.*

Small-group time is a good time to introduce materials and pieces of equipment that are specifically designed to *set in motion,* such as things with wheels, things that roll, things that spin, things that drip, and things that can be moved in a predictable path (swings, a merry-go-round, a seesaw, and so on). Such materials and equipment can help children experience and gain an awareness of direction and distance. See p. 39 for a summary list of these materials.

●●●●●●●●●▶ *Provide lots of opportunities for children to move.*

A true active learning environment and daily routine will provide an abundance of ways for children to move. In fact, a good way for you to assess the active learning quality of your setting is to look at the *freedom of movement* each part of the daily routine provides for children.

●●●●●●●●●▶ *Converse with children about positions, directions, and distances.*

Listen throughout the day for cues that may reveal children's thoughts about the positions, directions, and distances of things:

     Teresa (from the top of the climbing structure): *I'm higher up than you!*
Provide a supportive comment such as:

     Adult (looking up at Teresa): *You're way up there, aren't you!*

●●●●●●●●●▶ *Encourage children to explore their immediate environment.*

High/Scope's plan-do-review sequence provides a natural framework for children to experience and explore their immediate environment. As they follow their interests during work time, children will become involved with *positions* ("Here I am—under the table"), *directions* ("You wait over there and I'll run to you"), and *distances* ("I think the moon's 20 million hundred miles away"). Walks within the neighborhood will also provide children with opportunities to talk about directions and distances.

Key Experience

★ Interpreting spatial relations in drawings, pictures, and photographs

Young children often become very absorbed with looking at pictures, whether the pictures are photos of familiar people and places, book illustrations, or even drawings they have created. They may examine every spatial detail and then come to their own conclusions about how things relate, for example, which building seems taller or farther away.

Examples of children

Interpreting spatial relations in drawings, pictures, and photographs

- Felipe looks at the book The Flower Garden. When he reaches the illustration that provides an overhead view, he says, "I think this is how a spider sees them flowers." Shannon, the adult, replies, "That's how a spider would see the flowers?" Felipe responds, "Yeah, 'cause spiders can stick to the ceiling and see down."

- Thomas sits with a museum book in his lap, slowly turning the pages and looking intently at the paintings that interest him.

- Ellen looks at a series of pictures her teacher has taken during work time. "I made that," she says, pointing to the clay figure in one of the photographs. "But it's upside down!"

A well-stocked art area provides plenty of interesting materials for children to use with drawing or painting.

22

Ways to support children in interpreting spatial relations in drawings, pictures, and photographs

• • • • • • • • • ► *Provide a wide variety of pictorial materials.*

Choose pictorial materials that relate to children's experiences at home, in preschool, and in the community, as well as pictures that provide new experiences. Ideas include picture books, magazines, catalogs, photo albums, museum books, postcards from faraway places, and travel brochures.

• • • • • • • • • ► *Provide materials for children to use when making their own pictures.*

Keep the art area well-stocked with accessible materials so children can make their own drawings and find materials they may need for picture-making at recall and small-group time.

Book illustrations capture children's attention and offer many spatial details and relationships for them to think about.

• • • • • • • • • ► *Look at picture books with children.*

As you look at a book with a child and listen to his or her comments about the pictures, you can discover what attracts the child's attention and listen for references to spatial relations.

Take photographs of children in action.

A loaded or digital camera in the classroom is a wonderful tool for capturing pictures of children at work that can be shown to them later. For example, you might want to take a series of photographs of children building a structure and record the comments they make about positions and directions. Later, you can display the developed pictures for them with their comments written underneath.

These children will enjoy seeing pictures of the structure they have built with blocks, bottles, and steering wheels.

Key experiences in *time*

Preschoolers are just beginning to construct their own personal sense of time based on their active, sensory experiences. They may notice that a child has been away from the classroom for what seems like a long time, or they may remember that their birthday comes right after Thanksgiving vacation. Since they are able to keep mental images in mind, young children can remember and talk about things that happened in the past or will happen in the future, even though they still are focused primarily on the present.

Most preschoolers aren't ready to use clocks and calendars to mark the passage of time or to use terms like minutes, hours, and seconds accurately. Instead they express their ideas of time in ways that make sense to them:

• "I know it's nighttime 'cause the moon's up in the sky and it's dark out."

• "Pretty soon I'm going swimming with my grandma. When it's real hot out and I can wear my flip-flops."

Key Experiences in Time

★ Starting and stopping an action on signal

★ Experiencing and describing rates of movement

★ Experiencing and comparing time intervals

★ Anticipating, remembering, and describing sequences of events

This girl may discover that glue doesn't always stop pouring on signal!

Key Experience

★ Starting and stopping an action on signal

Starting and stopping an action on signal is a fun and concrete way for preschoolers to experience *time intervals.* On their own, children will often include *stop* and *start* commands in their group play by using timers, flashlights, musical instruments, or by clapping their hands. They also begin to notice that certain tasks have a beginning and an end, for example, popcorn pops slowly at first, speeds up, and then slows to a stop when all the popcorn is popped.

Examples of children

Starting and stopping an action on signal

- Anthony bangs the drum loudly as his classmates dance around the room. As he stops beating the drum, he yells "Stop!"

- Kumi and Lily watch popcorn popping in the corn popper and listen intently for the last pop. Kumi says, "It's done! Ummm, I love popcorn."

- Jessica turns the dial on a kitchen timer and tells Sahara, "When it dings, it's your turn."

Playing musical instruments while marching leads naturally to starting and stopping on signal.

Ways to support children in starting and stopping an action on signal

●●●●●●●●●▶ *Provide materials children can use to signal stopping and starting.*

Timers, musical instruments, tape recorders, and computer games are examples of materials that children can use to practice stopping and starting on signal. A more complete list of suggested materials is provided on p. 40.

●●●●●●●●●▶ *Let children know when time periods begin and end within the daily routine.*

A daily routine lets children regularly experience time intervals that stop and start in a consistent sequence. When children know the order of the daily routine, they can anticipate what's coming next, for

Blenders and popcorn poppers provide experiences with starting and stopping on signal.

example, they know that work time begins as each child starts his or her plan and ends five minutes after adults give a verbal five-minute warning.

●●●●●●●●●▶ *Sing, dance, and play musical instruments together.*

Children have a natural affinity for music and move readily to the beat. Combining movement and music activities during large-group time lets them experience starting and stopping on signal. For example, let children take turns being the instrument player and deciding when the rest of the children should stop moving.

●●●●●●●●●▶ *Watch for and support children's interest in stopping and starting.*

If you listen carefully, you will hear children use lots of stopping and starting language as they play. For example, you might hear a "train engineer" let his or her riders know when it's time to "get on board" the train and when to "get off" at the next station. As you listen, think of ways you might extend this activity and build on this interest, for example, by providing signal flags, an engineer's cap, train schedules, or a large bell.

★ Experiencing and describing rates of movement

In contrast to young toddlers who seem to run more than they walk, preschoolers enjoy their ability to purposefully regulate their activity speed. They also use their sizable command of language to describe rates of movement. You might hear them use words like *sneaking, creeping,* or *zooming* to describe how fast or slow something or someone is moving.

Examples of children

Experiencing and describing rates of movement

- Drew and Lorenzo are racing cars down a slanted race track they have created with blocks. "My car's the fastest," Lorenzo says. "Uh-uh. Mine is!" Drew replies.

- "You be the dog, and I'll walk you," Kara tells Nita. "Hurry up, doggie. You're so poky," Kara says. "We've got to get a move on."

- "I'm gonna learn to swim this summer. I'm going to swim fast like my sister!" Kevin says.

These boys see that some toy cars are slower than others.

28

Ways to support children in experiencing and describing rates of movement

•••••••••▶ *Provide materials children can set in motion.*

The list of materials that children can set in motion is nearly unlimited—large and small toys, playground equipment, furniture, and so on. See p. 40 for a list of materials to choose from for your setting. Many of the same motion-based materials that help children experience movement in space are also useful in helping them develop concepts about *time.*

•••••••••▶ *Provide opportunities for children to move at different rates.*

Some children complete activities very quickly and are ready to move on to the next experience. Others like to make the moment last and are more likely to linger in one area for quite a while. As you play music at cleanup time or

Movement and music activities at large-group time encourage children to move at different speeds and with different styles.

large-group time, include selections with varying tempos. Read or tell stories about children, animals, and vehicles moving at varying speeds and encourage children to act out and reproduce these rates of motion.

•••••••••▶ **Listen for and support children's observations about speed.**

Accept children's individual observations about speed. What is fast or slow to one child may seem quite the opposite to you or to other children. Although some elements of time are absolute (there are sixty minutes in an hour), part of being individuals is having our own sense of how long or short an experience seems.

<u>Key Experience</u>

★ Experiencing and comparing time intervals

Preschool children have a lively, subjective perception of time that is based on their own experiences, for example, waiting five minutes to have a turn on a tricycle may seem more like an hour. Remember that children's *perceptions* of each of the daily routine's predictable time intervals may be based more on their inner clock than on the wall clock—a 10-minute cleanup time will often feel much longer than a 30-minute outside time.

<table>
<tr><td>

Examples of children

**Experiencing
and comparing
time intervals**

• "Snack won't be for a
long time, and I'm hungry,"
says Theo.

• "I remember when we had
a robin's nest in our tree.
Maybe it will come back
again when the leaves
come out," Ramon reflects.

• "I wish nap time was as
fast as brushing my
teeth," Maria remarks.

</td></tr>
</table>

Children experience time intervals when waiting to go down the slide safely.

30

Ways to support children in experiencing and comparing time intervals

▶ *Relate lengths of time to familiar actions or events.*

When you cannot respond to a request right away, use concrete markers in your responses:

• "I'll come see your drawing when I finish listening to Maya's story."

• "As soon as all of the puzzles are put away, we'll be ready for recall time."

▶ *Provide sand timers for children to play with.*

Children quickly learn to use sand timers to define time periods that are meaningful to them—how much time before it's the next child's turn, how much time before they must "feed the baby," and so on.

Using a sand timer helps children take turns at the computer.

Key Experience

★ Anticipating, remembering, and describing sequences of events

A consistent daily routine gives children a sense of control over their lives by maintaining a regular set of communal activities against which they can think about time:

- "Large-group time is next, and then my mom comes."
- "It's almost snack time, and I get to pass out snacks today."

The High/Scope plan-do-review sequence is specifically designed to help children anticipate and recall work and play on a daily basis. Once you have established the daily routine, help children anticipate each period by warning them that the end of a time period is near, by signally the beginning and end of a time period, by asking children what comes next, and by giving a very short introduction (one or two sentences) to small- and large-group times so children will know what to expect.

Examples of children

Anticipating, remembering, and describing sequences of events

- "First my sister was born, then my brother, then me," recalls Robert.

- "I can't hardly wait till Halloween. Then it's my birthday, and I'm getting a new bike," states Demarcus.

- Laura says, "Remember when we went to the zoo that one time? That was so fun!"

With a consistent daily routine, children can anticipate what comes after cleanup time.

Ways to support children in anticipating, remembering, and describing sequences of events

▶ *Illustrate the order of daily events with children.*

Make up charts that help children see sequence—the parts of the daily routine, the steps in a recipe, the turns children will take for various chores. Use objects, photographs, pictures, or drawings to represent each step in the sequence.

▶ *Include living things indoors and outdoors.*

Living plants and animals in the classroom and outdoors offer children opportunities to observe growth and change. Keep a camera in the classroom so you can record stages of growth. Then find a creative way to present the pictures to children. For example, you could mark a 3-foot dowel at regular intervals with different colored markers and push the dowel into the soil next to something the children have planted. Take a picture every time the plant has grown past one of the colored marks and arrange the pictures in order on a large poster board. Children will enjoy seeing how the plant grew from the blue line to the red line to the purple line and so on.

Caring for living things and watching them grow is a concrete way for children to experience sequences of events.

▶ Look at seasonal change through preschooler's eyes.

Children often anticipate coming seasons and events in relation to what's happening with the weather. One might remember that his birthday is celebrated when there is snow on the ground or right after Halloween. Another might remember that her grandma comes for a long visit when it's warm enough to go to the lake. Relating meaningful events to the changing seasons lets children anticipate the upcoming event.

▶ Plan holiday celebrations around children's understanding of time.

Rather than planning holiday celebrations well in advance and providing activities and lessons in anticipation of the event, *let the special event emerge through children's conversations and actions.* Follow children's cues that they have heard parents and siblings talk about the upcoming event or seen stores changing their decorations in anticipation of the coming season. Right before and during the event, listen, observe, and interact with children to discover what they know about the event and the extent of their interest, and plan accordingly. After the event, expect to hear children living out the event again in the weeks or months to come.

Don't be surprised to see children talking excitedly about favorite events for weeks before and after they occur.

Space

★ **Filling and emptying**

___ Provide materials for filling and emptying.
   ___ Continuous materials for pouring
   ___ Discrete materials
   ___ A variety of containers and scoops
   ___ Computer software
___ Watch for and comment on children's filling and emptying play.
___ Imitate children's actions.
___ Anticipate repetition.

★ **Fitting things together and taking them apart**

___ Provide materials that fit together and come apart.
   ___ Commercial materials
   ___ Common household materials
___ Provide materials children can use to make their own things that fit together and come apart.
___ Provide time for children to work with materials on their own.
___ Support children as they solve fit problems.
___ At recall time, encourage children to talk about things they put together and took apart.
___ Include fit-together, take-apart materials at small-group time.

★ **Changing the shape and arrangement of objects (wrapping, twisting, stretching, stacking, enclosing)**

___ Provide materials to shape and arrange.
   ___ Blocks
   ___ Paper and cloth
   ___ Clay and dough
   ___ Rubber bands and elastic
   ___ Thread, string, yarn, ribbon, rope, wire, and pipe cleaners
___ Support children as they rearrange things to solve problems.
___ Listen for children's awareness of how they are shaping and arranging things.
___ Take cues from children to comment on changes they have made.

★ **Observing people, places, and things from different spatial viewpoints**

___ Provide sturdy play equipment.
   ___ Outside
   ___ Inside
___ Encourage children to crawl, roll, bounce, and lie on their backs.
___ Join children in a variety of positions.
___ Take walks with children.

* **Experiencing and describing positions, directions, and distances in the play space, building, and neighborhood**

___ Provide materials children can set in motion.

___ Provide lots of opportunities for children to move.

___ Converse with children about positions, directions, and distances.

   ___ Listen.

   ___ Comment.

   ___ Take directions from children.

___ Support children as they encounter and solve position problems.

___ Encourage children to explore their immediate environment.

   ___ Implement the plan-work-recall sequence.

   ___ Value cleanup time.

   ___ Go on walks with children.

* **Interpreting spatial relations in drawings, pictures, and photographs**

___ Provide a wide variety of pictorial materials.

___ Provide materials children can use to make their own pictures.

___ Provide opportunities for children to draw at recall time.

___ Display photos and drawings of block structures.

___ Look at picture books with children.

___ Take photographs of children in action.

   ___ Keep a loaded or digital camera handy.

   ___ Take photographs of the shaping and arranging process.

   ___ Take photographs from different spatial viewpoints.

   ___ Make photographs available to children.

   ___ Converse with children about the process and what they see from different perspectives.

Time

★ **Starting and stopping an action on signal**

___ Provide materials children can use to signal stopping and starting.
___ Let children know when time periods begin and end within the daily routine.
___ Sing, dance, and play musical instruments together.
___ Watch for and support children's interest in stopping and starting.

★ **Experiencing and describing rates of movement**

___ Provide materials children can set in motion.
___ Provide opportunities for children to move at different rates.
   ___ Play fast and slow music.
   ___ Re-enact stories that incorporate different rates of movement.
   ___ Encourage children to pour their own juice and milk.
___ Listen for and support children's observations about speed.

★ **Experiencing and comparing time intervals**

___ Establish and follow a consistent daily routine.
___ Relate lengths of time to familiar actions and events.
___ Accept children's observations about time.
___ Provide sand timers, kitchen timers, and stop watches for children to play with.

★ **Anticipating, remembering, and describing sequences of events**

___ Establish and maintain a consistent routine.
___ Help children learn the daily routine and anticipate what comes next.
___ At planning time, converse with children who are ready to make detailed plans.
___ Encourage children to recall events.
___ Illustrate the order of daily events with children.
___ Watch for children's sequenced representations.
___ Inform children about changes in the daily routine.
___ Include children in the change process.
___ Include living things indoors and outdoors.
___ Look at seasonal change through preschoolers' eyes.
___ Plan holiday celebrations around children's understanding of time.

Materials for Space and Time

Space

Materials for filling and emptying

- Indoor sand and water table
- Outdoor sandbox close to a water spigot or pump
- **Continuous materials for pouring:** sand, water, salt, and flour
- **Discrete materials:** small collections of things children can easily scoop up in their hands (small plastic animals, beads, poker chips, metal nuts, shells, stones, pea gravel, buttons, inch-cubes, and bottle caps)
- **A variety of containers and scoops:** cups, bowls, food storage containers, milk cartons and jugs, boxes, bottles, funnels, pails, buckets, crates, wagons, wheelbarrows, purses, suitcases, lunch boxes, bags, envelopes, spoons, trowels, shovels, and squeeze containers (turkey basters, plastic ketchup and mustard bottles, and so on)
- **Computer software drawing programs** that allow children to fill and empty the screen or parts of the screen with vivid colors they select. The bi-monthly *Children's Software Review* (*www. childrenssoftware.com*) contains many suggestions for appropriate software.

Materials for fitting things together and taking them apart

- **Commercial materials:** trucks and cars with removable parts, Tinkertoys, Lincoln Logs, interlocking blocks, snap-together trains and train tracks, pegs and pegboards, puzzles, slotted squares, parquetry blocks, beads and strings, Connecto-Straws, geoboards, dolls and doll clothes, markers and tops, staples and a stapler, a drill and drill bits
- **Common household materials:** all kinds of boxes; 35MM film canisters; jars and lids; pots and lids; plastic containers and lids; coffee percolators; plastic bottles and tops; screws and nuts; jewelry that clasps and snaps; keys on a key ring; and dress-up clothing that buckles, buttons, zips, and ties
- **Art materials:** paper products of any size and texture, including paper plates, grocery bags, greeting cards, and so on; painting and printing materials; fasteners such as hole punches, paste, glue, tape, pipe cleaners, wire, string, yarn, ribbon, shoelaces, threads, and needles with big eyes; collage materials; modeling and molding materials; and drawing and cutting materials
- **Woodworking materials:** safety goggles, claw hammers, saws, pliers, screwdrivers, vises, c-clamps, sandpaper, nails, golf tees, screws, nuts, bolts, washers, wood scraps, bottle caps and jar lids (for wheels), dowel-rod pieces

Materials for changing the shape and arrangement of objects

- **Blocks:** Unit blocks, large hollow blocks, cardboard brick blocks, small multi-colored blocks, inch-cubes, snap-together blocks, sandstone building blocks
- **Paper and cloth:** all kinds of paper and envelopes, along with fabric scraps, scarves, cloth napkins, towels, doll blankets, tablecloths, doll clothes, and dress-up clothes
- **Pliable materials** such as clay, dough, and beeswax that children can shape and re-shape through stretching, molding, and modeling
- **Stretchable materials** such as rubber bands and elastic that children can stretch or twist
- **Flexible materials** such as aluminum foil, thread, string, yarn, ribbon, rope, wire, and pipe cleaners that allow children to deal with the spatial complexities of twisting, looping, tying, and threading

Materials for observing people, places, and things from different spatial viewpoints

- **Sturdy outdoor equipment** that lets children climb and change position, such as swings, climbers, climbing nets, tree stumps, merry-go-rounds, ladders, hills, bridges, slides, tree houses, tunnels, seesaws, wheel toys, tricycles, scooters, a sand pile, and large inner-tubes
- **Sturdy indoor equipment** like large wooden blocks, heavy cardboard boxes, stools, a small stepladder, a rocking boat, and a hammock

Materials for experiencing and describing positions, directions, and distances in the play space, building, and neighborhood

- **Materials children can set in motion:** things with wheels, such as toy vehicles and ride-on toys; things that roll, such as balls, spools, beads, tubes, dowels, marbles, rings, and hoops; things that spin, such as tops, pinwheels, and board-game spinners; things that drip, such as water, paints, and glue; and outdoor equipment that can be moved in a predictable path, such as swings, a merry-go-round, and a seesaw

Materials for interpreting spatial relations in drawings, pictures, and photographs

- **Pictorial materials** related to their children's experiences at home, in preschool, and in the community, such as picture books, magazines, catalogs, photo albums, and computer software programs, as well as pictures that provide new experiences, such as museum books, postcards from faraway places, and travel brochures
- **Art materials** that children can use to make their own pictures
- **A camera,** loaded and ready to go, to take pictures of children throughout the day

Time

Materials for starting and stopping an action on signal

- Egg timers, sand timers, mechanical kitchen timers that tick and ring, alarm clocks, musical instruments, tape recorders and music tapes, and age-appropriate interactive computer games that call for stopping and starting actions on signal. The bi-monthly *Children's Software Review* (*www.childrenssoftware.com*) contains many suggestions for appropriate software.

Materials for experiencing and describing rates of movement

- **Materials children can set in motion:** things with wheels, such as toy vehicles and ride-on toys; things that roll, such as balls, spools, beads, tubes, dowels, marbles, rings, and hoops; things that spin, such as tops, pinwheels, and board-game spinners; things that drip, such as water, paints, and glue; rocking chairs and rocking horses; and outdoor equipment that can be moved in a predictable path, such as swings, a merry-go-round, and a seesaw
- **Computer software drawing programs** that allow children to draw and erase at whatever speed they wish. The bi-monthly *Children's Software Review* (*www.childrenssoftware.com*) contains many suggestions for appropriate software.

Materials for experiencing and comparing time intervals

- Sand timers, kitchen timers, and stop watches

Materials for anticipating, remembering, and describing sequences of events

- Charts that help children see sequence—the parts of the daily routine, the steps in a recipe, and the turns children with take for various chores
- Living plants and animals that provide children with opportunities to observe growth and change over a period of time
- Materials associated with particular seasons, holidays, and other special events

Related High/Scope® Resources

Classification, Seriation, and Number—Early Math

As young children explore their environment, they begin to notice relationships between similar things and to develop rules for treating things the same or differently, based on characteristics like color, size, shape, and texture. *Understanding these relationships and rules is the beginning of math learning.* This booklet and video provide strategies adults can use to encourage math exploration by recognizing and making the most of math learning opportunities throughout the day. Both the booklet and video are well illustrated with examples of children participating in math-related key experiences.

Book: BK-P1196 $9.95 Video: BK-P1197 $30.95 Set: BK-P1198SET $34.95

Book, soft cover, photos, 46 pages, 1-57379-139-3. Video, color, about 40 minutes, 1-57379-140-7.

Initiative and Social Relations

Young children are developing as independent decision makers who can make plans and carry them out and as community members who can form close relationships, play cooperatively, and show sensitivity and respect for others. They are becoming socially competent individuals. This booklet and video highlight strategies adults can use to support children in developing these key abilities. Children and teachers in a variety of High/Scope early childhood settings are featured. A checklist of teacher strategies is included. Colorful and informative!

Book: BK-P1181 $9.95 Video: BK-P1182 $30.95 Set: BK-P1183SET $34.95

Book, soft cover, photos, 32 pages. 1-57379-165-2; Video, color, 58 minutes. 1-57379-166-0

Language and Literacy

Using the ideas in this booklet and video, you can help preschoolers expand their conversational abilities and discover the usefulness and fun of the written word through six key experiences in language and literacy. The booklet includes both a list of materials for supporting early reading and writing and a teaching strategy checklist. The colorful, informative video features adults supporting and extending children's language and literacy experiences in actual High/Scope classrooms and centers.

Book: BK-P1155 $9.95 Video: BK-P1156 $30.95 Set: BK-P1157SET $34.95

Book, soft cover, photos, 28 pages. 1-57379-097-4; Video, color, 60 min. 1-57379-098-2

Creative Representation

Teachers, child care providers, and parents can use this easy-to-read booklet and companion video to learn how to recognize and support the six High/Scope key experiences in creative representation. Included are examples of how representation occurs in children's play, strategies for promoting representation, lists of materials that encourage representation, and a creative representation checklist.

Book: BK-P1146 $9.95 Video: BK-P1147 $30.95 Set: BK-P1148SET $34.95

Book, soft cover, photos, 28 pages, 1-57379-030-3; Video, color, about 40 min. 1-57379-087-7

To order these or any other High/Scope® products, contact High/Scope® Press: phone (800)40-PRESS fax (800)442-4FAX

To see a full listing of High/Scope® products, visit our Web site: *www.highscope.org*